Sacred Listening

Discovering God's Call for Your Life

Sacred Listening

Discovering God's Call for Your Life

Keith Clark-Hoyos

Sacred Listening: Discovering God's Call for Your Life

Scripture quotations are taken from the following translations:

- *New Revised Standard Version Updated Edition (NRSVue)*, © 2021 National Council of Churches of Christ in the United States of America. Used by permission. All rights reserved.
- *Contemporary English Version (CEV)*, © 1995 American Bible Society. Used by permission. All rights reserved.
- *New International Version (NIV)*, © 1973, 1978, 1984, 2011 Biblica, Inc.™ Used by permission. All rights reserved worldwide.

Printed in the United States of America.

ISBN: 979-8-9987673-5-7

Cover design: Keith Clark-Hoyos
Interior design: Keith Clark-Hoyos

Published by Clark-Hoyos Publications
Topeka, KS

For more resources, visit:
www.ChurchTrainingCenter.com

Dedication

To Zulima,

my beloved wife, whose unwavering support and steadfast partnership sustain every step of this calling.

Thank you for walking with me in the work, and for being my companion on this sacred journey of faith, love, and listening.

Books by
Keith Clark-Hoyos

Called Together: A Spirit-Led Discernment Guide for Congregational Planning

Embracing Our Call: A Practical Guide for Church Governing Body Leaders

The Ministry of Money: A Treasurer's Role in the Mission of the Church

Serving the Call: A Training Manual for New Governance Body Members

About the Author

Keith Clark-Hoyos is a dedicated leader known for his unwavering positivity and remarkable ability to guide and inspire within the realm of church leadership and administration. His life journey has been characterized by a deep commitment to personal and professional growth, a passion for teaching and coaching, and a profound love for nurturing individuals and organizations toward their highest potential.

In 2015, Keith transitioned from his role as a church judicatory leader to found Church Training Center — a thriving consulting, coaching, training, and accounting firm serving churches and nonprofits across the nation. Together with his wife and partner, he has built a team that supports mission-driven ministries with clarity, care, and Spirit-led wisdom.

Keith holds a Master of Arts in Ministry, Leadership & Service from Claremont School of Theology and an undergraduate degree in Business Administration and Church Ministries from Simpson University. He is also a Daoist Monk in the Wù Zhēn Pài (Awakened Reality Sect) lineage and brings a deeply contemplative and spiritually grounded presence to his work.

At the heart of Keith's calling is a desire to empower church leaders to live faithfully, lead effectively, and align all resources — financial, human, and spiritual — with the mission God has placed before them.

Table of Contents

Introduction:

The Way of Sacred Listening

Seeing Through a Dim Glass

"For now we see only a reflection, as in a mirror; then we will see face to face. Now I know only in part; then I will know fully, even as I have been fully known."

— 1 Corinthians 13:12 (NRSVue)

The life of faith is not a straight line, nor a list of answers, nor a set of formulas. It is, instead, a journey of listening. A journey of turning our hearts toward the Spirit who whispers in the quiet places, who guides us through Scripture and prayer, who reveals God's call not all at once, but step by step.

This book, *Sacred Listening: Discovering God's Call for Your Life,* is an invitation into that journey. Over nine weeks, you will be guided into practices of stillness, prayer, reflection, and discernment. Each week builds upon the last—surrendering, discovering identity, becoming like Christ, listening for your unique calling, clarifying vision, trusting God's seasons, stepping forward, releasing, and integrating what God has grown in you.

This is not a manual of quick fixes. It is not a self-help formula to engineer success. It is, instead, a sacred rhythm: a spiral of returning to God's presence, week after week, as you discover how to live more fully as God's beloved.

What Is Sacred Listening?

Sacred listening is the practice of opening ourselves to the voice of the Spirit. It is a way of being that trusts God's guidance more than our own striving, and God's timing more than our own urgency. It is choosing to believe that within us resides the Spirit's wisdom, waiting to be heard when we make room.

Sacred listening is not passive. It requires attention, trust, and courage. It is the act of setting aside the noise of culture and fear so we may hear the deeper voice that says, *"You are my beloved child. With you I am well pleased."*

You may already know this truth with your mind. Sacred listening helps you know it with your heart and embody it with your life.

As I look back on my own journey, I can see how hard it was for me to move beyond control. For years I was head-oriented, outcome-focused, and convinced that imposing my will was the most expeditious way forward. But ministry invited me to pause, listen, and allow space for God. Over time, I discovered that God works in the gaps and pauses, that true surrender means trusting the Spirit rather than mastering outcomes. I found God most clearly not in my analyzing and striving, but in stillness and emptiness—the very places I once resisted.

The Tools for the Journey

Sacred listening is supported by simple, practical tools. These are not formulas but companions for the journey. They create space to pause, reflect, and hold what the Spirit is stirring.

Along the way, I have learned that listening also requires tending to our most basic needs. We cannot hear clearly if we are exhausted, starving, or isolated. Just as our bodies need food, rest, play, and intimacy, our spirits need certainty, growth, contribution, connection, significance, and variety. When these needs are acknowledged and held before God, we are more ready to hear the Spirit's invitation.

This book provides simple tools you will return to again and again:

- **The Spirit's Basket**: a space to write down insights, nudges, or burdens during prayer and reflection. It is where you release what weighs you down and gather what the Spirit offers.
- **The Beloved in Christ Statement**: a personal declaration of who you are in Christ, built week by week. By the end of the journey, you will have a statement you can carry as an anchor for your identity and calling.
- **Weekly Practices**: Scripture readings, teachings, questions, prayers, and a "Mini-Examine" that help you notice God's presence each day.

These tools are not ends in themselves. They are companions to help you listen more deeply.

A Nine-Week Spiral

This journey unfolds over nine weeks, each building on the last:

1. **Surrender to Grace [Psalm 46:10]** — Learning to be still and let God fill the empty cup.

2. **Identity in Christ [2 Corinthians 3:18]** — Discovering who you are through God's reflection, not false mirrors.

3. **Becoming Like Christ [James 1:23–25]** — Allowing transformation to shape your actions and life.

4. **Personal Calling [Psalm 42:1]** — Following the thread of longing God weaves through your soul.

5. **Vision & Commitment [Revelation 3:20]** — Opening the door to God's vision and stepping into it with integrity.

6. **Season & Rhythm [Ecclesiastes 3:1–8]** — Trusting the wisdom of God's timing and rhythm.

7. **Spirit-Led Steps [Galatians 5:25]** — Taking concrete steps of faith guided by the Spirit's light.

8. **Release & Trust [John 3:8]** — Letting go of what you cannot control, carried by the Spirit's wind.

9. **Integration & Fruit [Galatians 5:22–23]** — Bearing fruit that reflects Christ's presence in your life.

Like a spiral, you may find yourself returning to earlier weeks. That is not failure but faithfulness. God often brings us back to surrender or identity so we can hear more deeply the second, third, or hundredth time.

The nine weeks that follow will guide you from surrender, to identity, to transformation, through calling and vision, into seasons of action, release, and fruit. These are not steps to master but rhythms to revisit again and again.

As I look back, I remember a season when this spiral became very real. After years in judicatory ministry, I spent months in prayer and meditation, listening for what was next. Everyone around me suggested another pastoral role, but it did not resonate with the Spirit's whisper in my heart. I sat in silence, listening, waiting, even interviewing for positions I knew were not mine. One evening, after months of uncertainty, I prayed for clarity. The next morning, I woke with a vision so clear it could not be ignored: the birth of Church Training Center. That clarity came only after surrendering fully — after I had let go of my insistence on the next obvious step. God's timing revealed what my striving never could.

Who Is This Book For?

This book is for anyone longing to listen more deeply to God. You may be:

- A person in transition, asking where God is calling you next.
- A leader seeking clarity for your service.
- A follower of Christ desiring a deeper spiritual rhythm.
- Someone weary of quick fixes and ready for Spirit-led guidance.

Whatever your starting point, you do not need prior experience in discernment. The Spirit meets you here.

How to Use This Book

Each week offers:

- A **Scripture anchor** to ground your reflection.

- A **Teaching** to frame the theme.

- A **Tool** to practice sacred listening.

- **Prompts & Exercises** for journaling and reflection.

- A **Prayer** to center your heart.

- A **Spirit's Basket page** to gather insights.

- A **Mini-Examine** to review your day.

- A **Spiral Return reminder** to revisit themes as needed.

- A **Closing Reflection** to mark the week's gift.

You can move through one chapter each week, or linger longer if the Spirit calls. The journey is yours with God.

The Tone of the Journey

This is not about striving but surrender. Not about achieving but abiding. Not about forcing answers but creating space to hear.

Throughout these nine weeks, you are invited to listen sacredly—to trust that the Spirit is already at work in you, and that God's call is not something to invent but to discover.

Closing Invitation

Sacred listening is not about reaching a final destination, but about walking faithfully in step with the Spirit. Each week, you will discover something new — not to finish the journey, but to deepen it.

I've come to see that calling is rarely a single endpoint. Often it is a challenge or lesson, a place where God grows us for what lies ahead. The journey itself is the destination. As Philippians 1:6 promises, "The one who began a good work among you will bring it to completion by the day of Christ Jesus." With each step of listening, you become more of who God created you to be.

A Prayer for Beginning

Holy God, I open myself to You. Quiet my striving and awaken my listening. Teach me to hear Your Spirit's whispers, to trust Your guidance, and to discover the call You have woven into my life. May this journey of sacred listening draw me deeper into Christ, and may it bear fruit for the good of the world. Amen.

Week 1:

Surrender to Grace

"Be still, and know that I am God."

— Psalm 46:10 (NRSVue)

Additional supporting scriptures:

"My grace is sufficient for you, for my power is made perfect in weakness."

— 2 Corinthians 12:9 (NIV)

"Do not conform to the pattern of this world, but be transformed by the renewing of your mind."

— Romans 12:2 (CEV)

Teaching: Beginning with an Empty Cup

Every journey of sacred listening begins not with control, but with surrender. Scripture reminds us that God's presence and calling are revealed when we step away from striving and open our hearts to the Spirit.

Psalm 46:10 anchors this truth: *"Be still, and know that I am God."* Stillness is not passivity—it is an act of courage to lay down the illusion that we can master life by effort alone. When we surrender, we create space for God to speak.

This phase is like an empty cup before God, ready to receive God's grace. Discernment is not about chasing outcomes or following self-help formulas; it is about abiding with the Spirit, trusting that God's grace fills the space our striving vacates.

As Paul reminds us in 2 Corinthians 12:9, God's power is made perfect in weakness. By emptying ourselves, like an open cup, we allow God's Spirit to pour in. Romans 12:2 echoes this: transformation comes through renewal, enabling us to discern God's will.

Consider Mary, who sat at Jesus' feet listening while Martha hurried (Luke 10:39–42). Jesus affirmed Mary's choice, teaching that surrender—choosing the "better part"—prepares us to hear His call. This week, you are invited to emulate her: not to do more, but to be still. Surrender is not giving up; it is opening up, trusting God knows your path.

As you release the noise of daily demands, the Spirit whispers your unique calling, a journey that unfolds gently over these nine weeks.

Personal Reflection: *When I was discerning my next steps in ministry, everyone assumed the obvious path was another called role. I kept interviewing and praying, yet something in me felt misaligned. For months I sat in silence, surrendering my need to decide and asking only to be led. There were no instant answers—only the invitation to trust.*

Then, after a long season of waiting, clarity came in a single morning: a vision for Church Training Center. Looking back, I can see the clarity did not arrive until I had truly let go of forcing an outcome. Surrender was not giving up; it was opening up—so the Spirit could reveal what striving never could.

Tool: The Spirit's Basket

This week, begin using your **Spirit's Basket**—a place to write down insights, nudges, scriptures, or burdens. Capture anything that arrives during your time of listening.

_____

_____

_____

_____

_____

_____

_____

_____

_____

_____

_____

Voice Discernment Guidance: Test what you place in the Basket against scripture and the peace in your heart. What aligns with God's love will deepen peace and clarity.

Prompts & Exercises

1. Where in your life do you feel invited to surrender?

2. What distractions keep your cup from being empty before God?

3. Write down one thing you feel called to release this week to deepen your sacred listening. Place it in your Spirit's Basket and pray over it.

Exercises

- **Stillness Practice**: Spend five minutes in silence each day. Begin with the breath prayer: *"Holy Spirit, empty me to receive Your whispers."*

- **Release Exercise**: Identify one burden to set aside each day. Place it in your Basket as an offering.

Prayer

Holy God, help me to be still and know You are God. Empty my striving and fill me with Your presence. Teach me to surrender to grace, to open my heart, and to listen sacredly. Amen.

Spirit's Basket — Week 1

Date: _____

Sacred Listening Notes:

Burdens released: _____

_____

_____

Whispers noticed: _____

_____

_____

Scriptures that anchor: _____

_____

_____

Mini-Examine

Calling: *Where did I sense God's invitation today?*

Energy: *How did I spend my energy? Was it drained or renewed?*

Resources: *Did I use the gifts and resources entrusted to me faithfully?*

Discernment: *Did I pause to listen before acting, or did I rush ahead?*

Offer these reflections back to God in a closing prayer.

8

Spiral Return

Return to this week whenever life feels cluttered or overwhelming. Sacred listening begins again with the empty cup.

Closing Reflection

Week 1 opens the journey with surrender. By emptying yourself before God, you make space for grace. The Spirit is faithful to fill what you release.

Week 2:

Identity in Christ

"And all of us, with unveiled faces, seeing the glory of the Lord as though reflected in a mirror, are being transformed into the same image from one degree of glory to another; for this comes from the Lord, the Spirit."

— 2 Corinthians 3:18 (NRSVue)

Additional supporting scriptures:

"So God created humankind in his own image, in the image of God he created them."

— Genesis 1:27 (NIV)

"You are a chosen people, a royal priesthood, a holy nation, God's special possession."

— 1 Peter 2:9 (CEV)

Teaching: Seeing with Unveiled Faces

Week 1 invited you to begin with surrender. Now the Spirit invites you to look in the mirror—to see yourself not through distortions of culture, fear, or shame, but through the glory of Christ reflected in you.

Paul writes that with unveiled faces, we are being transformed into the image of Christ. Sacred listening reveals your identity in God's call. Each time you turn your gaze to Christ, you discover who you truly are—not by comparison, not by accomplishment, but by God's love.

This phase is like a mirror with many reflections, revealing the multifaceted glory of Christ. Mirrors show us what is visible and what lies hidden. Spiritually, they remind us that identity is not static but transforming— reshaped as we behold Christ.

The world offers false mirrors: *You are what you own. You are your success or failure. You are what others think.* But the Spirit offers a different reflection: *You are my beloved child.*

Mary sat at Jesus' feet because she knew her true worth was not in proving herself but in being loved and taught by Him. Sacred listening invites you to that same stillness, where your identity is defined by Christ alone.

Personal Reflection: *There have been seasons when I tried to define myself by how much I could produce or endure. Once, while meeting with judicatory leaders, I learned my brother was being placed in hospice. My instinct was to keep working, to push through, and to deal with my grief later. I shared briefly what was happening, almost apologizing for my distraction.*

But those leaders stopped me. They gathered around, prayed with me, and set aside their agenda so I could have space to grieve and breathe. In that moment, they reflected back to me who I truly am: not a role, not productivity, but a beloved child of God. Their compassion reminded me that identity is not in what I accomplish, but in Christ who calls me beloved.

Tool: The Spirit's Basket

Use your Basket to collect truths about your identity. Write down scriptures or affirmations that reflect who you are in Christ.

_____

_____

_____

_____

_____

_____

_____

_____

_____

_____

_____

Voice Discernment Guidance: Ask: _Does this reflection deepen love and peace? Does it align with the truth of being God's beloved?_

Prompts & Exercises

1. How have false mirrors shaped your view of yourself?

2. What reflection of God's image do you long to believe more fully?

3. Begin your "Beloved in Christ Statement" with: *"I am a beloved child of God who..."*

Exercises

- **Mirror Exercise**: Stand before a mirror and repeat: *"With unveiled face, I see Christ shaping me."*
- **Scripture Writing**: Copy Genesis 1:27 or 1 Peter 2:9 by hand and keep it nearby this week.

Prayer

Jesus Christ, You are the mirror in which I see my true self. Strip away the false reflections that leave me anxious or ashamed. Teach me to listen sacredly, that I may live as Your beloved child, created in Your image. Amen.

Spirit's Basket — Week 2

Date: _____

Sacred Listening Notes:

Burdens released: _____

_____

_____

Whispers noticed: _____

_____

_____

Scriptures that anchor: _____

_____

_____

Mini-Examine

Calling: *Where did I sense God's invitation today?*

Energy: *How did I spend my energy? Was it drained or renewed?*

Resources: *Did I use the gifts and resources entrusted to me faithfully?*

Discernment: *Did I pause to listen before acting, or did I rush ahead?*

Offer these reflections back to God in a closing prayer.

Spiral Return

Return here when you forget who you are. Sacred listening brings you back to your true reflection.

Closing Reflection

Week 2 affirms your identity in Christ. You are not what the world says. You are God's beloved, ever being transformed.

Week 3:

Becoming Like Christ

"For if any are hearers of the word and not doers, they are like those who look at themselves in a mirror; for they look at themselves and, on going away, immediately forget what they were like. But those who look into the perfect law, the law of liberty, and persevere—being not hearers who forget but doers who act—they will be blessed in their doing."
— James 1:23–25 (NRSVue)

Additional supporting scriptures:

"Do not be shaped by this world; instead be changed within by a new way of thinking."

— Romans 12:2 (CEV)

"This is my prayer: that your love may abound more and more in knowledge and depth of insight."

— Philippians 1:9–10 (NIV)

Teaching: Transformation at the Stream

Week 1 began with surrender. Week 2 revealed your identity in Christ. Now, in Week 3, sacred listening invites you into transformation— becoming more like Christ in the rhythms of daily life.

This phase is like the clear surface of a stream, reflecting Christ's image when we are still. When disturbed, the reflection blurs. Likewise, transformation requires stillness to behold Christ clearly—and courage to let His image shape our actions.

James warns that it is possible to look in the mirror and immediately forget who you are. Forgetting happens when we hear the Word but do not embody it. Sacred listening is not merely about receiving God's voice but responding in daily life.

Paul echoes this in Romans 12:2: transformation flows from renewal, not conformity. Philippians 1:9–10 adds that love must abound in wisdom and discernment. Transformation is never abstract—it takes shape in relationships, choices, and commitments.

This sacred listening shapes you into God's call. You are not asked to become someone else, but to become more fully yourself in Christ.

Personal Reflection: *As an entrepreneur, I have often looked for wisdom from experts. Many systems promised success, especially in marketing, but their tactics relied on creating urgency and manipulating decisions. I quickly realized those approaches did not reflect what the Spirit had taught me about discernment.*

Churches make decisions slowly, in prayer, and as a community. To adopt strategies built on pressure would mean conforming to the world rather than being transformed by Christ's way. I had to choose: follow "best practices," or embody the pattern of sacred listening. Transformation meant rejecting what seemed effective and trusting God to shape my work in a way aligned with grace.

Tool: The Spirit's Basket

Use your Basket to record moments of transformation—times when you acted differently because of sacred listening.

_____

_____

_____

_____

_____

_____

_____

_____

_____

_____

_____

_____

Voice Discernment Guidance: Ask: _Does this action align with Christ's teaching? Does it bear peace, love, or wisdom?_

Prompts & Exercises

1. When have you forgotten your reflection in Christ?

2. What small action could reflect Christ more fully this week?

3. Update your "Beloved in Christ Statement" by adding: "...*and growing in Christ's likeness.*"

Exercises

- **Mirror of Action**: Choose one scripture to live out today. Write it in your journal, then note in the evening how you embodied it.
- **Release of Resistance**: Name one way you resist Christ's shaping. Write it down and prayerfully release it.

Prayer

Christ Jesus, shape me into Your likeness. Do not let me forget who I am, but help me to live as one who hears and responds. Teach me to listen sacredly, that transformation may take root in my life. In Your peace, I rest. Amen.

Spirit's Basket — Week 3

Date: _____

Sacred Listening Notes:

Burdens released: _____

_____

_____

Whispers noticed: _____

_____

_____

Scriptures that anchor: _____

_____

_____

Mini-Examine

Calling: *Where did I sense God's invitation today?*

Energy: *How did I spend my energy? Was it drained or renewed?*

Resources: *Did I use the gifts and resources entrusted to me faithfully?*

Discernment: *Did I pause to listen before acting, or did I rush ahead?*

Offer these reflections back to God in a closing prayer.

Spiral Return

Return to this week whenever faith feels abstract. Sacred listening grounds transformation in action.

Closing Reflection

Week 3 affirms that transformation is possible. By staying still before Christ and acting in response to His Word, you become more fully who God created you to be.

Week 4:

Personal Calling

"As a deer longs for flowing streams, so my soul longs for you, O God."
— Psalm 42:1 (NRSVue)

Additional supporting scriptures:

"Before I formed you in the womb I knew you, before you were born I set you apart."

— Jeremiah 1:5 (NIV)

"Each of you should use whatever gift you have received to serve others, as faithful stewards of God's grace in its various forms."

— 1 Peter 4:10 (CEV)

Teaching: The Thread That Pulls You Forward

Week 1 began with surrender. Week 2 affirmed your identity. Week 3 called you into transformation. Now, in Week 4, sacred listening leads to discovering your **personal calling**—the unique way God invites you to live out love and service.

This phase is like a thread woven by God, gently pulling you toward God's purpose. Calling is not only about what you do, but about who you are in Christ and how your gifts meet the world's needs.

Psalm 42:1 gives voice to this longing: just as a deer longs for streams, so our souls long for God. This longing often shows up as desire, restlessness, or a deep pull that cannot be ignored.

Jeremiah 1:5 reminds us God's call begins before birth—woven into our very being. And 1 Peter 4:10 urges us to use our gifts for others, as stewards of grace. Calling is both deeply personal and always oriented toward love and service.

Sacred listening is not about comparing your calling to another's. It is about listening to the thread that pulls you forward, trusting that God is weaving your life into the larger story of redemption.

Personal Reflection: *When I was discerning my next step in ministry, everyone assumed the obvious path was another called role in judicatory leadership. I kept interviewing, listening, and praying, yet something in me felt misaligned.*

For months, I sat in silence, surrendering my need to decide and asking only to be led. No instant answers came—only the invitation to trust. Then, one morning after a long season of waiting, I awoke with a vision so clear it could not be ignored: the birth of Church Training Center.

Looking back, I can see that clarity did not arrive until I had truly let go of forcing an outcome. Calling often begins as longing, and God's thread tugs us forward in ways we cannot predict. My surrender prepared me to receive what striving never could.

Tool: The Spirit's Basket

This week, use your Basket to write down glimpses of your calling: nudges, longings, or gifts others affirm in you.

_____

_____

_____

_____

_____

_____

_____

_____

_____

_____

_____

_____

Voice Discernment Guidance: Ask: _Does this thread pull me toward love, service, and peace?_

Prompts & Exercises

1. What longings or restlessness do you feel when you listen for God?

2. What gifts or passions have others affirmed in you?

3. How might these be signs of calling?

Exercises

- **Thread Exercise**: Write down three desires you feel drawn to. Pray over them, asking the Spirit to reveal which threads lead to God's purpose.
- **Beloved in Christ Statement**: Add, *"...and called to a unique purpose in God's story."*

Prayer

Holy One, You created me with intention and care. Help me to listen sacredly for the thread that pulls me toward my calling. Guide me to trust that Your purpose for me is good, and give me courage to follow. Amen.

Spirit's Basket — Week 4

Date: _____

Sacred Listening Notes:

Burdens released: _____

_____

_____

Whispers noticed: _____

_____

_____

Scriptures that anchor: _____

_____

_____

Mini-Examine

Calling: *Where did I sense God's invitation today?*

Energy: *How did I spend my energy? Was it drained or renewed?*

Resources: *Did I use the gifts and resources entrusted to me faithfully?*

Discernment: *Did I pause to listen before acting, or did I rush ahead?*

Offer these reflections back to God in a closing prayer.

Spiral Return

Return to this week whenever you feel restless or uncertain. Sacred listening reveals calling as a thread God weaves through your life.

Closing Reflection

Week 4 affirms that you are created with purpose. God has planted a longing within you—a thread to follow in trust.

Week 5:

Vision & Commitment

"Listen! I am standing at the door, knocking; if you hear my voice and open the door, I will come in to you and eat with you, and you with me."
— Revelation 3:20 (NRSVue)

Additional supporting scriptures:

"Write the vision; make it plain on tablets, so that a runner may read it."

— Habakkuk 2:2 (NRSVue)

"Let your 'Yes' be yes and your 'No,' no."

— Matthew 5:37 (NIV)

Teaching: The Doorway of Vision

Sacred listening reveals not only who you are but what God invites you to commit to. Vision is the Spirit's gift of clarity. Commitment is your faithful response.

This phase is like a doorway opening to God's vision, inviting you to step through. The knocking is Christ's presence, asking for your openness. Revelation 3:20 reminds us that God does not force entry; the invitation is yours to answer.

Habakkuk 2:2 tells us to make the vision plain. God's invitations often come as glimpses—pictures, words, or inner clarity that require writing down to be remembered.

Commitment transforms vision into action. Jesus' words in Matthew 5:37 remind us that faithful living requires integrity: saying yes where God calls and no where God does not.

Sacred listening at this stage asks: *What vision has God shown me? What commitments will sustain it?*

Personal Reflection: *In my work, people often carry expectations of what they believe I should do. Over time, I've learned that anytime "should" shows up, it is rooted more in expectation than in Spirit-led clarity.*

A wise mentor once told me, "Expectations are premeditated disappointments. Lower your expectations. Raise your standards." That counsel continues to guide me.

When situations arise where a client expects something from me outside of what we agreed, I can stand firmly in who God says I am, rather than in their disappointment. I return to the standards we share, clarify them, and raise them together so that we both understand and commit to them.

God's vision is not found in other people's expectations but in faithful standards rooted in prayer, Scripture, and calling. Opening the door to that vision means choosing faithfulness over "should."

Tool: The Spirit's Basket

Write down any visions you sense—images, words, or prayers. Then note one commitment that could make this vision real.

_____

_____

_____

_____

_____

_____

_____

_____

_____

_____

_____

_____

Voice Discernment Guidance: Ask: _Does this vision align with God's love? Does it draw me deeper into Christ's way?_

Prompts & Exercises

1. What vision is God placing before me in this season?

2. What commitment could I make to live into that vision?

3. What would stepping through the doorway look like?

Exercises

- **Vision Statement**: Write a short statement of the vision you sense God calling you toward.
- **Commitment Exercise**: Name one step of faithfulness you can commit to this week.

Prayer

Christ who knocks, help me to hear Your voice and open the door. Give me vision to see where You are leading and courage to commit my life to it. May my yes be clear and my no be faithful. Amen.

Spirit's Basket — Week 5

Date: _____

Sacred Listening Notes:

Burdens released: _____

_____

_____

Whispers noticed: _____

_____

_____

Scriptures that anchor: _____

_____

_____

Mini-Examine

Calling: *Where did I sense God's invitation today?*

Energy: *How did I spend my energy? Was it drained or renewed?*

Resources: *Did I use the gifts and resources entrusted to me faithfully?*

Discernment: *Did I pause to listen before acting, or did I rush ahead?*

Offer these reflections back to God in a closing prayer.

Spiral Return

Return here when vision grows cloudy or commitments feel heavy. God's invitation is patient and faithful.

Closing Reflection

Week 5 affirms that vision and commitment are sacred gifts. Listening opens the doorway, and stepping through with faith makes vision real.

Week 6:

Season & Rhythm

"For everything there is a season, and a time for every matter under heaven."
— Ecclesiastes 3:1 (NRSVue)

Additional supporting scriptures:

"Teach us to number our days, that we may gain a heart of wisdom."

— Psalm 90:12 (NIV)

"Come to me, all you that are weary and are carrying heavy burdens, and I will give you rest."

— Matthew 11:28 (CEV)

Teaching: Seasons of God's Rhythm

Sacred listening unfolds not in a single moment but across seasons. To listen well is to recognize the rhythm of God's timing.

This phase is like the seasons of God's rhythm, flowing through time with purpose. Ecclesiastes 3 reminds us there is a time for everything: birth and death, planting and harvest, weeping and laughing. Seasons teach us to trust God's wisdom in timing.

Psalm 90:12 invites us to number our days—to see them as sacred. Matthew 11:28 assures us that rest itself is holy, not wasted. Rhythm means embracing both activity and stillness.

Sacred listening at this stage asks: *What season am I in? What rhythm is God inviting me to follow?*

Personal Reflection: *When I first began experimenting with time management systems, I realized many were misaligned with the Spirit's rhythm of discernment. In adapting one for myself, I discovered I had actually written the foundation of* Called Together, *a discernment guide for churches. I had never planned to write a book, yet clarity came when I paused long enough to notice the Spirit's timing.*

I've also learned that seasons of waiting can be unexpectedly fruitful. When COVID shut everything down in California, my consulting and training schedule disappeared overnight. It was a barren season for Church Training Center, yet in that space, Zulima and I refined our accounting systems and embraced new opportunities like online cohort training. What first felt like loss became a season of preparation.

Discernment is rarely linear. Sometimes clarity arrives suddenly, pulling everything else into the background. Other times the Spirit nudges us gradually. Over time, I've come to see that even the sharp turns in my path have been part of a larger rhythm, moving me steadily toward my calling.

Tool: The Spirit's Basket

This week, write down the season you believe you are in. What rhythms of work or rest feel Spirit-led?

_____

_____

_____

_____

_____

_____

_____

_____

_____

_____

_____

_____

Voice Discernment Guidance: Ask: _Does this rhythm bring me closer to peace in Christ?_

Prompts & Exercises

1. What season of life am I experiencing?

2. How do I resist or embrace this season?

3. What rhythm would honor God in this time?

Exercises

- **Season Chart**: Draw four quadrants—planting, growing, harvesting, resting. Place your current life season within one.
- **Beloved in Christ Statement**: Add, *"...and trusting God's seasons to guide me."*

Prayer

Holy Spirit, teach me to honor the season I am in. Help me embrace Your rhythms of work and rest. Give me peace to walk in time with You. Amen.

Spirit's Basket — Week 6

Date: _____

Sacred Listening Notes:

Burdens released: _____

_____

_____

Whispers noticed: _____

_____

_____

Scriptures that anchor: _____

_____

_____

Mini-Examine

Calling: *Where did I sense God's invitation today?*

Energy: *How did I spend my energy? Was it drained or renewed?*

Resources: *Did I use the gifts and resources entrusted to me faithfully?*

Discernment: *Did I pause to listen before acting, or did I rush ahead?*

Offer these reflections back to God in a closing prayer.

Spiral Return

Return here when life feels rushed or uncertain. Sacred listening restores rhythm through God's seasons.

Closing Reflection

Week 6 affirms that life unfolds in sacred rhythm. Seasons shift, but God's Spirit remains faithful, guiding you through each one.

Week 7:

Spirit-Led Steps

"If we live by the Spirit, let us also be guided by the Spirit."
— Galatians 5:25 (NRSVue)

Additional supporting scriptures:

"Your word is a lamp to my feet and a light to my path."

— Psalm 119:105 (NIV)

"Trust in the LORD with all your heart and lean not on your own understanding; in all your ways acknowledge him, and he will make straight your paths."

— Proverbs 3:5–6 (CEV)

Teaching: Steps of Faith

Sacred listening leads to action. After surrender, identity, transformation, calling, vision, and rhythm, the Spirit now invites you to take concrete steps forward.

This phase is like a path beneath your feet, lit by the Spirit for each step. Galatians 5:25 reminds us that life in the Spirit is not only inward but outward—choices, commitments, and movements that embody faith.

Psalm 119:105 affirms that God's Word lights the path, step by step. And Proverbs 3:5–6 calls us to trust God's direction, not our own limited understanding.

Sacred listening is not about knowing every step ahead, but about taking the next faithful one.

Personal Reflection: *When my mentor passed away, I remembered his challenge to me:* learn to take action. *As someone who tends to live in my head, I often hesitated, analyzing instead of moving. To honor him, I joined a mindset group and promised myself I would do whatever the leader asked—burpees, cold showers, daily exercise, sharing my story. These simple acts became lessons in surrender. Even the smallest "yes" became practice for the larger yeses the Spirit would one day ask of me. The will itself is a muscle; the more we exercise it in trust, the more prepared we are to say yes when it matters most.*

At times I've also learned what happens when I act too quickly, assuming I know where God is leading. When I impose my will, things do not flow. Obstacles multiply, and I'm reminded to pause and listen again. Paradoxically, the greater my faith, the less clarity I seem to have about the future. Each day is its own surrender, trusting God for the next step, not the whole path.

I once worked with a church whose leaders faced the possibility of closure. They gathered courage to present four options, including merging with another congregation. The members voted to merge—though no partner church existed yet. Their decision was not a plan, but a Spirit-led step. Over time, their discernment deepened. What began in uncertainty became a unifying act of faith. They didn't know the full path ahead, but they had learned to trust the Spirit enough to take the next step together.

Tool: The Spirit's Basket

Write down steps you sense God inviting you to take this week. They may be small, like reaching out to someone or beginning a new habit of prayer.

_____

_____

_____

_____

_____

_____

_____

_____

_____

_____

_____

_____

Voice Discernment Guidance: Ask: _Does this step lead me toward Christ's way of love and peace?_

Prompts & Exercises

1. What step of faith am I being nudged to take?

2. What fears keep me from moving forward?

3. How do I recognize the Spirit's light on the path?

Exercises

- **Next Step Practice**: Write one clear step you can take in the coming week. Pray over it and place it in your Basket.
- **Beloved in Christ Statement**: Add, "*...and walking faithfully in Spirit-led steps.*"

Prayer

Guide me, O God, in the steps You set before me. Teach me to walk in trust, even when the path is unclear. May my choices reflect Your Spirit's light. Amen.

Spirit's Basket — Week 7

Date: _____

Sacred Listening Notes:

Burdens released: _____

_____

_____

Whispers noticed: _____

_____

_____

Scriptures that anchor: _____

_____

_____

Mini-Examine

Calling: *Where did I sense God's invitation today?*

Energy: *How did I spend my energy? Was it drained or renewed?*

Resources: *Did I use the gifts and resources entrusted to me faithfully?*

Discernment: *Did I pause to listen before acting, or did I rush ahead?*

Offer these reflections back to God in a closing prayer.

Spiral Return

Return here when you feel stuck. Sacred listening reminds you that the Spirit lights each next step.

Closing Reflection

Week 7 affirms that sacred listening always leads to action. Trust the Spirit to guide each faithful step.

Week 8:

Release & Trust

"The wind blows where it chooses, and you hear the sound of it, but you do not know where it comes from or where it goes. So it is with everyone who is born of the Spirit."
— John 3:8 (NRSVue)

Additional supporting scriptures:

"Cast all your anxiety on God, because he cares for you."

— 1 Peter 5:7 (NIV)

"Into your hands I commit my spirit; you have redeemed me, O God of truth."

— Psalm 31:5 (CEV)

Teaching: A Holy Letting-Go

Sacred listening is not only about holding on to vision and steps. It is also about release—trusting God when the future is unclear.

This phase is a holy letting-go, trusting the Spirit's wind to carry you. John 3:8 reminds us the Spirit moves mysteriously. We cannot control it. Our role is trust.

1 Peter 5:7 assures us that God cares for us and receives our anxieties. Psalm 31:5 teaches us to place our lives in God's hands.

Sacred listening often brings us to a point of surrender—not to weakness, but to deep trust.

Personal Reflection: *Several years ago, after receiving the Covid vaccine, my body reacted in ways I could not control. My liver and kidneys were affected, and for months my health was fragile. I am someone who likes to act, plan, and push forward — but in that season there was nothing I could "fix." I had to release control and live one day at a time.*

In the quiet of that struggle, I learned that trust is not just believing God is present when life feels good; it is surrendering to God's care when nothing is certain. Healing came slowly, not through my effort, but through letting go of urgency and receiving the grace of each small improvement.

That long season became a teacher. It forced me to learn how to care for myself in ways I had neglected: eating congruently with my body's needs, honoring the impact of exercise, rest, and sleep, and supporting my health through supplements and self-awareness. What began as a frightening loss of control became a doorway into a healthier, more grounded way of life.

I discovered again that the Spirit moves like the wind — unseen, unpredictable, yet carrying us toward life. Releasing control opened me to trust, and trusting led me into a way of living more in tune with God's gift of body and Spirit.

Tool: The Spirit's Basket

Write down what you sense God inviting you to release. Place each burden, fear, or plan into your Basket as an offering.

_____

_____

_____

_____

_____

_____

_____

_____

_____

_____

_____

_____

Voice Discernment Guidance: Ask: _Does releasing this bring deeper trust, freedom, and peace?_

Prompts & Exercises

1. What am I clinging to that God invites me to release?

2. What fears arise when I think of letting go?

3. What trust would releasing this deepen in me?

Exercises

- **Release Exercise**: Each day, write one thing you commit to God's care. Tear up the paper or place it in your Basket as a sign of surrender.
- **Beloved in Christ Statement**: Add, *"...and learning to release what I cannot control."*

Prayer

Spirit of God, teach me to let go. Help me release what I cling to and trust that Your wind carries me. May surrender bring me peace and deepen my sacred listening. Amen.

Spirit's Basket — Week 8

Date: _____

Sacred Listening Notes:

Burdens released: _____

_____

_____

Whispers noticed: _____

_____

_____

Scriptures that anchor: _____

_____

_____

Mini-Examine

Calling: *Where did I sense God's invitation today?*

Energy: *How did I spend my energy? Was it drained or renewed?*

Resources: *Did I use the gifts and resources entrusted to me faithfully?*

Discernment: *Did I pause to listen before acting, or did I rush ahead?*

Offer these reflections back to God in a closing prayer.

Spiral Return

Return here when control feels heavy. Sacred listening deepens when you release.

Closing Reflection

Week 8 affirms that letting go is holy. Trust the Spirit's wind to carry what you cannot.

Week 9:

Integration & Fruit

"By contrast, the fruit of the Spirit is love, joy, peace, patience, kindness, generosity, faithfulness, gentleness, and self-control. There is no law against such things."
— Galatians 5:22–23 (NRSVue)

Additional supporting scriptures:

"And this is my prayer: that your love will keep on growing and that you will fully know and understand how to make the right choices."

— Philippians 1:9 (CEV)

"Remain in me, as I also remain in you. No branch can bear fruit by itself; it must remain in the vine."

— John 15:4 (NIV)

Teaching: Fruit That Lasts

The nine weeks of sacred listening—surrender, identity, transformation, calling, vision, rhythm, steps, and release—culminate here in integration and fruit.

Galatians 5:22–23 describes the fruit of the Spirit. These are not goals we achieve; they are evidence of God's Spirit growing within us.

Philippians 1:9 prays that love will keep growing and shape wise choices. John 15:4 reminds us that fruitfulness comes only from remaining in Christ.

This phase is about integration—bringing together all that has been discerned into a life that bears fruit. Sacred listening becomes daily practice, shaping who we are and how we live.

Personal Reflection: *As I look back on my journey of discernment, I can see how the Spirit has been weaving fruit through my life in ways I could not have planned. When I founded Church Training Center, I thought the fruit would be measured in outcomes — successful systems, financial clarity, better leadership structures. Over time, I learned the real fruit is not what I accomplish, but what is formed in me and in those I serve.*

Patience grew when clarity took months to come. Gentleness grew when I discovered others needed me to pause and listen rather than press forward. Joy grew not from achievements, but from walking alongside leaders who rediscovered their own callings. Even peace grew, though often in the middle of struggle, as I learned to trust that God was at work beyond what I could see.

Integration is not a final product — it is the ongoing weaving of these fruits into our daily life. For me, that has meant recognizing that everything I teach about sacred listening must be embodied in my own choices: how I respond to stress, how I treat my body, how I engage with my family, and how I lead in ministry. The fruit of the Spirit is not just evidence of God's presence; it is also the sustenance that carries us into the next season of calling.

Tool: The Spirit's Basket

Use your Basket to gather evidence of fruit: moments of love, joy, peace, or patience. Note where kindness, generosity, or faithfulness grew.

_____

_____

_____

_____

_____

_____

_____

_____

_____

_____

_____

Voice Discernment Guidance: Fruit grows slowly. Ask: *Is this Spirit's fruit or my striving?*

Prompts & Exercises

1. Which fruit of the Spirit do I see most in my life?

2. Which fruit feels most in need of growth?

3. How does staying rooted in Christ help me bear fruit?

Exercises

- **Fruit Journal**: Each day, record where you saw Spirit's fruit.
- **Beloved in Christ Statement**: Add, *"...and bearing fruit that blesses others."*

Prayer

Holy God, integrate all I have learned through sacred listening. Grow Your fruit in me—love, joy, peace, patience, kindness, generosity, faithfulness, gentleness, and self-control. Keep me rooted in You, that my life may bless others. Amen.

Spirit's Basket — Week 9

Date: _____

Sacred Listening Notes:

Burdens released: _____

_____

_____

Whispers noticed: _____

_____

_____

Scriptures that anchor: _____

_____

_____

Mini-Examine

Calling: *Where did I sense God's invitation today?*

Energy: *How did I spend my energy? Was it drained or renewed?*

Resources: *Did I use the gifts and resources entrusted to me faithfully?*

Discernment: *Did I pause to listen before acting, or did I rush ahead?*

Offer these reflections back to God in a closing prayer.

Spiral Return

Return here often. Integration is lifelong, and the Spirit continually bears fruit.

Closing Reflection

Week 9 affirms that sacred listening bears lasting fruit. Stay rooted in Christ, and your life will reflect love.

Conclusion:

From Me to We

Sacred listening is never finished. What began as a nine-week journey through stillness, reflection, and prayer does not end here; it continues, unfolding in the rhythm of your days and in the life of the community you are part of. These weeks have been a spiral of return: circling deeper into the truth that God is always speaking, always calling, always drawing you into greater love.

We began with surrender. Week 1 invited you to lay down striving and receive grace, to hold yourself like an empty cup before God. Stillness became your first teacher: "Be still, and know that I am God" (Psalm 46:10, NIV).

In Week 2, you gazed into the mirror of Christ, seeing yourself as beloved, created in God's image, and being transformed from glory to glory (2 Corinthians 3:18, NRSVue). Your identity was not found in what you own, accomplish, or fear, but in God's unshakable love.

Week 3 invited transformation. Listening became more than hearing—it became embodying. James urged us not to forget what we see in the mirror of God's word but to live it (James 1:23–25, NRSVue). Transformation flowed from stillness into action, from reflection into response.

In Week 4, the thread of personal calling pulled at your heart. Like the psalmist longing for the living God (Psalm 42:1, NIV), you began to recognize that your life holds a unique shape in God's purpose. Your call is not another's; it is your own sacred way of being and serving.

Week 5 carried you to the doorway of vision and commitment. Revelation reminded us that Christ stands at the door and knocks (Revelation 3:20, CEV). To open the door is to welcome vision and responsibility, to choose the path of discipleship not once, but again and again.

Seasons and rhythms followed in Week 6. Ecclesiastes reminded us that everything has its appointed time (Ecclesiastes 3:1, NRSVue). Sacred listening is not hurried. It is a rhythm of rest and action, silence and speech, waiting and moving. God works through seasons, shaping you with patience.

Week 7 called you to Spirit-led steps. "Since we live by the Spirit, let us keep in step with the Spirit" (Galatians 5:25, NIV). Each step mattered, even the smallest ones. The Spirit illumined the path beneath your feet— not all at once, but enough to keep moving faithfully.

Week 8 invited release and trust. Like the wind Jesus described in John 3:8 (NRSVue), the Spirit is free, uncontained, moving in ways we do not predict. Sacred listening meant loosening your grip, letting go of illusions of control, and trusting the Spirit to carry you forward.

Finally, Week 9 gathered the fruits of the Spirit—love, joy, peace, patience, kindness, generosity, faithfulness, gentleness, and self-control (Galatians 5:22–23, NRSVue). These were not achievements of willpower but gifts of grace, signs of Christ being formed in you. Integration was not the end of the spiral but the beginning of a life shaped by listening.

Living the Tools

Along the way, you practiced tools meant to anchor sacred listening beyond these pages. They remain with you as companions for the journey:

- **The Spirit's Basket** gave you a way to gather insights, nudges, burdens, and gratitudes. Each entry was a reminder that God speaks through whispers as well as longings. As you continue, let this basket never close. Return to it when you sense new stirrings. Hold what you hear, test it against scripture, and let peace confirm its truth.
- **The Beloved in Christ Statement** reminded you daily of who you are: beloved, created in love, being transformed, and called with purpose. Words shape us. Let your statement continue to grow with you. Speak it aloud when you doubt yourself. Write it on your heart until it becomes the truest mirror you see.
- **The Mini-Examine** gave you a way to pause, even for a few minutes, to ask: Where did I sense God's call? How did my energy flow? What resources did I steward faithfully? Did my choices align with love? These small pauses, repeated, shape a life of discernment.

Together, these tools are not tasks to complete but practices to embody. They are seeds that will bear fruit as you use them again and again.

From Me to We

Sacred listening begins within, but it does not end there. The Spirit calls us into community, into a body that is larger than ourselves. Personal discernment becomes the foundation for communal discernment.

94

The apostle Paul reminds us that "to each is given the manifestation of the Spirit for the common good" (1 Corinthians 12:7, NRSVue). Your listening matters not only for your own growth but for the flourishing of the whole body of Christ. What you have learned in stillness becomes wisdom for your family, your congregation, your neighborhood, and your world.

This is the movement from *me* to *we*. You listened to discover your identity, your calling, your transformation. Now the invitation is to bring that listening into shared spaces. Churches need people who pause before they speak, who pray before they act, who discern together what the Spirit is saying. The world needs disciples whose decisions are shaped by love, not fear.

From me to we means recognizing that your story joins a greater story. You carry your thread into a tapestry woven by the Spirit. Each time you surrender, claim your belovedness, and embody God's call, you strengthen the fabric of the community around you.

Personal reflection: *To stay grounded in sacred listening, I have learned to honor both body and spirit. We hear more clearly when basic needs are tended—rest, nourishment, play, and healthy connection—alongside the deeper needs of the heart: belonging, growth, contribution, meaning, and joy. When these are held prayerfully before God, our lives become more receptive to the Spirit's guidance. I have also learned that calling is rarely a destination. More often it arrives as a lesson, a stretch of love, a faithful step that prepares the next. The journey itself is the point. I trust the promise that the good work begun in us will be brought to completion in Christ's time. Our choice each day is whether to resist and be dragged along, or to surrender and walk in communion with the Spirit—listening, responding, and becoming who we are created to be.*

Encouragement for the Road

As you continue, remember this: sacred listening is not about arriving. It is about returning. The spiral is endless, because God's voice is endless. Each day is another chance to surrender, to see yourself in Christ, to be transformed, to follow your call, to open the door, to honor the season, to walk in step, to release, and to bear fruit.

When you forget, return. When you falter, return. When you rejoice, return. Each return is welcomed by grace.

Philippians 1:6 (NRSVue) offers this assurance: *"The one who began a good work among you will bring it to completion by the day of Jesus Christ."* You are not alone in this journey. God's Spirit is faithful. The work begun in you will continue to grow, in you and through you.

So go gently, listening with your whole heart. Let silence be your teacher. Let scripture be your guide. Let the Spirit's nudges direct your steps. And let your life become a witness—not of striving, but of love.

This book ends, but the listening continues. Carry with you the tools, the reflections, and the practices you have discovered. Share them with your community. Let sacred listening become the way you live, the way you lead, the way you love.

And as you move forward, may you always hear the whisper of God's voice, calling you deeper into life, deeper into grace, deeper into the joy of Christ's presence.

Afterword:

The Journey Continues

The nine weeks of sacred listening you have walked are not the end of the journey but the beginning of a lifelong rhythm. Each time you pause to listen, surrender, and trust, you enter again into the spiral of grace.

Yet discernment is never only individual. The Spirit calls us into communities where our listening can be woven together into a shared song. When a congregation listens together, God's vision emerges in new and surprising ways.

If you feel stirred to carry this practice beyond your own life, consider stepping into the communal journey. *Called Together* offers a pathway for churches to practice sacred listening as one body. *Embracing Our Call* guides governing bodies in aligning their leadership with God's purpose. *The Ministry of Money* equips treasurers and finance leaders to see their work as a sacred ministry.

Church Training Center also nurtures leaders through the **Effective Church Leadership Community (ECLC),** a gathering place for those seeking wisdom, courage, and Spirit-led clarity in governance and stewardship. Here, leaders learn, share, and walk alongside one another as they discover how God is calling their communities forward.

Your journey of sacred listening continues — in your own heart, in your home, and in your faith community. May the Spirit's whisper guide you, and may you discover again and again that God's call is both deeply personal and beautifully shared.

Continue the Journey

Your nine-week journey of sacred listening is only the beginning. God's call continues to unfold in your life and in your community. To support you, Clark-Hoyos Publications and the Church Training Center provide resources that help leaders and congregations listen faithfully, govern wisely, and steward resources with integrity.

Effective Church Leadership Community (ECLC): An online hub for leaders to explore discernment, governance, and stewardship together. Inside the ECLC you'll find webinars, templates, discussion forums, and opportunities for ongoing formation.

Join the Effective Church Leadership Community

https://community.churchtrainingcenter.com/plans/1897267

Further Reading: Explore additional books and resources on the next page, each designed to deepen your practice of Spirit-led leadership and discernment.

Cohorts and Training: Join others in small groups for guided practice, conversation, and learning. These experiences offer space to integrate sacred listening into the rhythms of leadership and community.

You are not alone in this journey. The Spirit calls us forward together, and the Church flourishes when we listen as one.

If You Have Discerned You Are Ready to Lead…

Some who complete this journey of sacred listening will feel a nudge toward leadership. If you sense the Spirit inviting you to serve your community in new ways, you do not walk alone.

For those entering or deepening their leadership, Clark-Hoyos Publications offers resources to guide your steps. *Embracing Our Call* supports governing body leaders with practical wisdom rooted in discernment. *The Ministry of Money* reframes the treasurer's role as a sacred ministry of stewardship. *Serving the Call* equips new officers and board members for faithful service.

Alongside these resources, the **Effective Church Leadership Community (ECLC)** provides an ongoing space of support. Through shared learning, webinars, and practical tools, leaders across traditions gather to strengthen one another and listen for the Spirit's guidance in their work.

If you have discerned readiness for leadership, take the next step with prayer and courage. Explore these resources, seek community, and remember always that leadership is not about position but about faithfulness to the call of God.

Additional Resources

Available at churchtrainingcenter.com/publications/

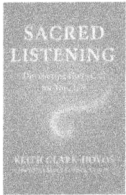

Sacred Listening
Discovering God's Call for Your Life
An invitation to discern your personal calling through sacred listening practices.

Called Together
A Spirit-Led Discernment Guide for Congregational Planning
A nine-phase pathway for churches to listen for God's voice and align mission with Spirit-led calling.

Embracing Our Call
A Practical Guide for Church Governing Body Leaders
Helps church leaders center their governance in God's call, with clarity, courage, and grace.

The Ministry of Money
A Treasurer's Role in the Mission of the Church
Reframes the treasurer's work as a spiritual ministry of stewardship, guided by Romans 12:8.

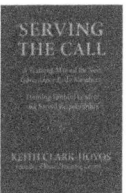

Serving the Call
A Training Manual for New Governance Body Members
Equips officers and board members to lead faithfully, grounding practical tools in spiritual discernment.

Tools for Sacred Listening

The Spirit's Basket

The Spirit's Basket is a place to hold the gifts and stirrings you receive in prayer. It creates space to notice God's presence, release burdens, and gather gratitude.

How to Use:

Quiet yourself with a breath prayer.

Record what arises as you listen — insights, nudges, burdens, gratitude.

Use this page often; return to it as a living record of your listening.

_____

_____

_____

_____

_____

_____

_____

_____

_____

_____

_____

_____

_____

_____

_____

_____

_____

_____

_____

_____

_____

_____

_____

_____

_____

_____

_____

_____

_____

Voice Discernment Guidance:

Test what you've written against Scripture and the peace of the Spirit. God's voice will always align with love, truth, and grace.

Beloved in Christ Statement

Your Beloved in Christ Statement is a living affirmation of your identity in God. Throughout these nine weeks, you have been invited to add to it — beginning with the truth that you are God's beloved child, and expanding as you discern your calling, gifts, and fruits.

How to Use:

Review the pieces you've written week by week.

Bring them together into a single, flowing statement.

Rewrite and refine it as your journey continues — God's Spirit may add new words in different seasons.

Example:

I am a beloved child of God, created in love, growing in Christ's likeness, called to a unique purpose, trusting God's seasons to guide me, walking faithfully in Spirit-led steps, learning to release what I cannot control, and bearing fruit of peace.

_____

_____

_____

_____

_____

_____

_____

_____

Mini-Examine

Purpose

The Mini-Examine is a short daily prayer practice to help you notice how your life is aligning with God's call. It centers on four questions that reflect the pattern of Calling–Energy–Resources–Discernment.

How to Use

Set aside 3–5 minutes at the end of the day.

Quiet yourself, and briefly answer the questions below.

Keep your answers simple — a few words or sentences.

Offer what you notice back to God in prayer.

Questions

Calling: Where did I sense God's invitation today?

Energy: How did I spend my energy? Was it drained or renewed?

Resources: Did I use the gifts and resources entrusted to me faithfully?

Discernment: Did I pause to listen before acting, or did I rush ahead?

Mini-Examine

Calling: *Where did I sense God's invitation today?*

Energy: *How did I spend my energy? Was it drained or renewed?*

Resources: *Did I use the gifts and resources entrusted to me faithfully?*

Discernment: *Did I pause to listen before acting, or did I rush ahead?*

Offer these reflections back to God in a closing prayer.

Rule of Life – Quarterly Check

Purpose

To sustain sacred listening, it helps to pause every few months and realign your life with your calling.

How to Use

Look back at your Spirit's Basket, Beloved in Christ Statement, and Mini-Examine entries.

Where is God calling me now?

_____

_____

_____

_____

_____

_____

How is my energy being spent?

_____

_____

_____

_____

_____

_____

What resources need attention?

_____

_____

_____

_____

_____

_____

What practices deepen discernment?

Commit to 2–3 small practices for the next quarter (e.g., more silence, intentional relationships, new rhythms of prayer).

_____

_____

_____

_____

_____

_____

_____

_____

_____

Scripture Index

A Final Word

Sacred listening does not end with this book. It continues each time you pause, breathe, and open your heart to God.

Carry forward what you have begun: the stillness of surrender, the joy of identity, the courage of calling, the fruit of the Spirit.

You are God's beloved. You are called. You are sent.

May your days be guided by the Spirit's whisper, and may your life bear witness to the One who calls you by name.